The Growth of a Girl to the Wisdom of a Woman

The Growth of a Girl to the Wisdom of a Woman

My Life's Emotional Etchings

Stephanie Olivia Bell

This book tells a fictional story taking place far into the future. The content reflects the expression of the author's ideas and opinions, and not necessarily those of the publisher.

Copyright © 2021 by Stephanie Olivia Bell.

All rights reserved. No part of this book may be reproduced, transmitted, or distributed in any form by any means, including, but not limited to, recording, photocopying, or taking screenshots of parts of the book, without prior written permission from the author or the publisher. Brief quotations for noncommercial purposes, such as book reviews, permitted by Fair Use of the U.S. Copyright Law, are allowed without written permissions, as long as such quotations do not cause damage to the book's commercial value. For permissions, write to the publisher, whose address is stated below.

Printed in the United States of America.

ISBN 978-1-953150-64-6   (Paperback)
ISBN 978-1-953150-65-3   (Digital)

Lettra Press books may be ordered through booksellers or by contacting: Lettra Press LLC
30 N Gould St. Suite 4753 Sheridan, WY 82801
1 307-200-3414 | info@lettrapress.com www.lettrapress.com

IN LOVE, YOUNG AND HOPEFUL

My Life's Emotional Etchings

THE KISS

*Your kiss rests gently
on my lips,
as the morning dew upon
the rose.
Sweetly clinging through
the day,
a reminder of your
loving ways.*

*As evening forms and
your arms encircle me,
the morning kiss
is fanned to a burning flame,
deep as the setting sun.*

*As I slip into your
waiting arms,
the strength and passion
of your kiss
is fuel enough 'til next
your lips meet mine,
in the gentle dawn of morning.*

AFTER

*There is something definitive
permeating my being.*

*It wasn't so clear
when you were here.*

*But now it posseses,
infusing my senses.*

*It's in my hair,
my taste, my skin.*

*It's you, your essence,
the nector of your being.*

I shall never bathe.

MY SMILE

*I lie in pure exhaustion
with a grin from ear to ear.
My smile ascends to loving eyes
and knows that you are here.*

*And yet, upon departure,
my smile continues on.
It comes from somewhere deep inside,
and steadily it grows.*

*It glows, it flows throughout my being,
until I seem to walk about
wrapped in sunshine, safe, secure;
immersed in smiles, so warm, so sure.*

And all because of you.

SELF-AWAKENING

*Through your love of me,
I finally see
myself, my soul, my body,
and know their beauty.*

*Because of yesterday,
today I dance and smile.
today I hope and right,
and melt a lot.*

*Two weeks of dreams.
They went too fast.*

MY SONG

I don't really sing in the morning.
I don't really sing in the day.
But today,
I sang in the morning,
and all for yesterday.

I don't often sing in the evening.
I rarely sing in my sleep.
But tonight,
my dream was a song,
and all for yesterday.

Yesterday was my dream,
will still stay my dream
today,
if I sing for you.

Yesterday was a song,
the birds sang along.
The willow ceased to weep.

BROWN EYES

Fluid,
Liquid,
Moulton,
Dark;
Deep,
Brown,
Syrup;
Luminous,
Clear and
Soft,
Brimming full,
your eyes.

THE CALL

*Outside
the moon is full;
so too my eyes,
for the sorrow in my heart
spills forth unchecked.*

*Through my blurred and misty vision,
the moon seems dim.
Pale and watery it becomes.
There is no solace there.
I wander back inside.*

*But then you call.
"Thank you love.
I too will be thinking of you,
and you'll be by my side.
Goodnight my love."*

*Outside
the moon is full;
so too my heart,
with love for you
those twinkling stars cannot outshine
nor distance soon diminish.*

YOU ARE THE RAINBOW

*You are the rainbow
in my day.
Grey skies and clouds
just pass away.*

*My smile begins
when you walk in.
And with your calls,
my dormant heart
begins to beat.*

ANOTHER CALL

I awoke early.
I called you
to continue my dream.
Fantasy, interwoven with reality:
blending wishes with memories.

Which is which?
Which was?
Which will be?
You're ever in my thoughts,
forever in my heart,

and thus it will be
until at last,
we are together again.

A SPECIAL CALL

*The memory of hearing
your soft, sleepy, cozy morning voice
rolling out of the phone,
has been a special place
I visit through my day.
You awaken a dormant heart,
sstir the caldron of blood in my veins,
warming, heating it into a pulsing stream,
rushing to the far reaches of my body.*

*You cannot begin to know
how sacred ae these moments.*

*I try to keep perspective,
but every now and then I weaken.*

*May God keep us safe 'til next we meet;
and you gather and enfold me
in your strong, loving arms.*

LONGING

*I have
an insatiable thirst
for you;
like*

*the first gulp of
the first cold beer;*

*like
the sun drenched summer ground at
the first splash of rain,
I have this thrist for you.*

*I want to drink your juices,
to kiss your mouth, your ear,
the small of your neck.*

*I want to melt into you;
to be absorbed by your face,
your body, your arms.*

*I have
this thirst for you.*

Can it ever be quenched?

YOU HAVE GONE

*I am wrapped in the
smell of the phone;
the gaze of your eyes;
the warmth of your arms;
the touch of your hands;
the pulse of your heart;
the petals of your roses.*

*Surely your goodness,
your love,
your excitement,
your passion,
your tenderness,
your thoughtfulness,
energy and surprises*

*will enfold me
in your absent times.*

3 AM IN THE MORNING

awoke
basking in the warmth
of our call;
your words
swirling round
my head.

Lying
in the glow
of memory,
I wander through the years.

I wonder,
no, I marvel at the power.
I am sustained
by thoughts, pictures,
phone calls.

Is the power
and energy of my
imaginataion that real?
Can I last
in this fantasy
another year?

*As a child
growing up,
I never had a
make-believe friend.
Is that what
you have become?*

*I think not;
for you are real.
"make-up" nothing,
just relive everything,
and pray tomorrow
will soon be yesterday.*

THE MOON NOT FULL

*Half a moon
is half of me.
You're gone,
and half of me
is half of thee.*

*The moon is full
on your returns,
as is my heart,
my soul, my arms
of you.*

TIME

*You're ever on my mind,
forever in my heart.
Why, oh why are we apart?*

*TIME, that precious and elusive commodity,
the only non-markeetable product, must be
spent to be savored, cannot be stored.*

*For if stored, changes its' qualities-now
becoming PATIENCE, which can only endure a
certain lifespan, else it too changes its' structure,*

*Soon to become DESPAIR, and despair too long
endured becomes the DEATH of TIME.*

*TIME in order to be remembered, must be spent
and savored, and nurtured to flourish.*

Please, let us spend some TIME together, soon.

ADDICTION

Oh my God.
I thought I had it licked!
Will I never learn?
Does it take a slap in the face,
a bloody fire
to burn out the passion and flame in my heart?

Does this have to run its course?
Do I have to hit bottom
for it to end,
to have it be over,
forever over?

for it not to come creeping back,
to fllicker and flame again;
roaring through me,
consuming me night and day,
burning me up.

Oh my God
Please, help me to put this fire out.
It is not one that helps re-growth.
It's out of control,
running unchecked
leaving waste and ruin in its path.

*Please, help me channel this,
to focus elsewhere.
This cannot be love.
It hurts too much.
Help me find a love
that will grow through mutual
energies expended.*

*If I were to measusre the time of
thought, word and deed
devoted to this addiction, and been repaid in kind,
I could have a love made iin Heaven.
I feel your absence in this and it is Hell.*

I NOW SEE

*I now see
you cannot yet
love me with abandon.
I need to be
loved with abandon,
joy and amazement.*

RECOVERY FROM A DEEP HURT

Sleep,
the soothing balm of sorrow.
Sun,
it's bandage.
Time,
the healer.
Indulge,
they're all God's gifts.

REMEMBER

*When the sun warms
the dew on the rose,
remember.*

*When the warmth from it's rays
lengthen the days,
remember.*

*When the splashing sea sparkles
with the light from above,
remember.*

*When the moon takes over
so the sun can rest,
remember.*

*And I'll remember
for you are
still the sun to me.*

I REMEMBER HIM

*On this first September morn,
where the touch of Fall was evident
through milkweed turned a subtle rust,
and cool residue of air settling
on the canyon floor,
I remembered him.*

*From the first splash
of spilled water on my
journal at dawn,
to the last wave lapping
the shore at dusk,
I remembered him.*

*Is now the time?
Are healing hearts a lifelong process?
Will I wake some morn
and say, "I'm well,
my heart is whole again?"*

*Is now the time to let him go?
Two years to the day
he went his way.
The hole in my heart is
smaller now.
Perhaps it stays,
so I'll remember him.*

WONDER

*A Crescent moon,
a tiny star.
And I wonder
How you are?*

UNDERSTANDING

My Life's Emotional Etchings

DAWN

The day and I awake together.
As the clouds cover the sky,
so too the mist of sleep fills my eyes.

The early morning birds
begin to sing and speak.
I too feel motion stir my body
as I stretch and yawn,
my eyes still closed.

I sense, rather than see
the beginnings of light.

THE BRANDY ROSE

*Like brandy held in a bottle,
the rose held in the hand of love
passed on in friendship,
opens and warms the heart.*

*The second day, just as she said,
the rose started to unwind.
Nestled in its leaves,
it settled in.*

*Captured on an opening petal,
two dewdrops.
I stared in wonder.*

*Could it be instead
drops of nectar
left, perhaps, by a a hummingbird?*

*Like the budding burst of youth.
Now unfolding into adulthood,
settling against its pillows,
(having spent its life to the
full potential God intended),*

*bringing
joy and beauty
to the beholder:*

The "Brandy Rose"

*And so it was.
The day finally came
when the rose laid open
the last petal upon her
bed of green support.*

*Lying unfurled,
practically flat,
her inner soul exposed,
I waited.*

*And still I wait,
as petals close in upon themselves,
never loosing the
pale soft glow of tangerine.*

*When it arrived,
the rose had no special perfume.
It was as if the fragrance
was housed inside.*

Once it started unfolding,
the wafts of perfume
spilled forth.

And on the 10th day
of its arrival,
the "Brandy Rose"
wilted in perfection.

Each softly layered petal
resting on itself,
each with a rim of curling color.

Unlike other roses,
the "Brandy" hangs onto its petals,
none fall off.
No water is consummed.

It isn't till later, I realize the rose is dead.

AFTER THE STORM A WALK ON THE BEACH

*Cool whip, meringue and marshmellows
from the churning sea;
cast upon the shore all three.
"Floating Island" on the
custard ofreceding waves.
Shinning sugar sparkling.
White floaty clouds
swoop down to kiss the foam,
linking sky and sea.
Brisk, wet winds
push them back again;
black sky into blue.
he storm has passed.
The day will last.
Memories will prevail.*

MY MOON

*Full moon,
quietly sitting,
not racing as before.*

*Last night
you were so resless
streaking through the clouds.
Couldn't get a chance to talk.
You were so busy
playing hide and seek.*

*Tonight is better.
You're very quiet,
Absolutely still.*

*But tonight,
I have nothing to say.*

MY DRIVE HOME

Sharply crystaled,
clear as ice;
finely etched
upon the clouds,
the mountains loom.

And as the clearing winds subside,
night's lights sparkle on the valley floor.
Above,
a mirror of equal strength
reflecting the sky's stars.

GOD'S MAJESTY

*Soaking wet hair,
pale Autumn body
sitting in the winter sun.*

*Swathed, bathed, buried in
raining white flowering
pear blossoms,*

*shocked into release by the
sudden Santana winds.
The present balmy breezes*

*pushing the clouds from
the soaring sun,
rising quickly now*

*so as to set on time;
soon to pass across the space
where the morning's setting moon
lingered over Malibu.*

All this in a day.
A dawn to
a rapidly gathering sunset.

My vista spans all four corners
as I perch upon my mountain top.
Nature to the right of me,
freeway to the left.

Multicolored billowing clouds,
mountain peaks and valleys,
fog banks,
beginning stars.

The sounds, the smells,
the sparkling lights,
cause me such delight.
God's majesty abounds.

IN MEMORY

*One white as snow
with a bud still forming.
The other blush rose
of remembered cheeks.*

*One year has passed
since her passing;
but her memories linger
in her growing garden.*

*Her rosess bring pleasure
to neighbors and friends;
keeping her always alive.
For giving them care,
she is there for you*

THE GARDNER

spray,
pestilence abounds.
I water,
dichondra withers.
Vegetation arise.
Let's call a truce.
Unfair my thumb to call
black, but green it isn't.
Perhaps puce?

THE WHITE ROSE

*The white rose
of winter.*

*He said it was
the last.*

*Creamy white
it was,*

*A bud
just opening.*

*I watched it
through the week.*

*Wider and wider
it became.*

*Spreading it's petals
until at last,*

*all were gathered
round the vase.*

*The white rose
joining the circle
of fallen beauty.*

*Imparting no more
pleasure
to the eye of the beholder.*

*Just a memory.
The last white rose
of winter.*

FAITH AND WISDOM

My Life's Emotional Etchings

TRANSITION

From your floating bed of air,
softly suspended;
soothed and wrapped
with wafting warm breezes,
'til God floats you to
the waiting clouds of Heaven,
I'll pray for you.

AFTER I'M GONE

I shall not send red roses.
A bouquet of memories
will be my gift to you.

Frail as dandelions gone to seed;
or happy as bright daffodils.
Some with the sweetness and newness of baby's breath;
or vibrant, lasting and strong as the rose.

Memories filled with surprise;
like finding a crocus popping through the snow.
Some hanging with the heavy scent of musk;
others romantic and lingering as gardenias.

You see I cannot send the roses.
My bouquet of memories
is my gift to you.

EDNA LILLICH DAVIDSON LUNCHEON SALONS

Each face I explore,
as the book review progresses,
is filled with captured stories;
stories waiting to be released.
The incredible depth of
personal anguish,
reflecting memories long forgotten,
yet mirrored in the deep lines
and glistening eyes
spills forth.

What a wealth of stories untold.
What an untapped resource,
a life, those lives, my life,
yours and mine.
We all are walking books.
Time and patience,
effort too
must be employed to just begin to know
a chapter or two of each other.
Let's begin our reading soon.

HOPE ETERNAL

The sky was navy blue.
She was old, old, old,
yet her heart had not wrinkled.
Silver spray splashed
upon her face.
The sun shot through
her sleeping form.
Drifting, dreaming
as when young.

Fragile now and frail
as cobwebs.
Foaming bubbles
on the waves.
She woke slowly
life still before her.
Well and whole,
a spirit willing.
Only time and age
her foe.

SHE CAUGHT IT

*60 years of negotiated living
have not left me totally inept.
When the master of ceremonies of
the after-wedding festivities announced:
"Alright, all the single girls and women
come to the dance floor.
The bride is about to toss her wedding bouquet.
Who will be the lucky winner?"*

*Wow, what an invitation!
In that the bride had married her personal trainer,
and a good many of his "customers" were [resemt
(all married),,
I did not have that contingency to
muscle in on the action.*

*So, I proceeded to the dance floor.
Of course, going up to the bride in advance and
hissing in her ear:
"you owe me one,"
had absolutely nothing to do with the results!*

*Be it noted, however,
I was able to leap over the 12 year old flower girl
(niece of the bride)
and grab the bouquet as it sank to the floow,
rising to the applause of all,
Wedding Bouquet held high and
no sign of the intended in sight.*

NOW I UNDERSTAND

*It's only in aloneness
one has time to ponder,
to evaluate, to create.*

*It's only by yourself
appreciation of another
comes to bear.*

*It's only in the joining,
concentric circles that we are,
that we are at peace.*

FRIENDS

Have you friends
silent as stone?
Others that glow, gush and flow?
Some perhaps may quietly roam,
while neighbors carp, bicker and moan.
Have you a friendly, bubbling friend,
enthused, embued with quiet confidence?
Which friend are you
to all your friends?

DO YOU LIVE WITH SOMEONE?

Do you live with someone?
Yes, but it's not a problem.
He keeps his place, is very neat. Doesn't
communicate or interfere unless I initiate it.
What's nice is when I get home late,
he is almost always there;
a warm friendly presence.
A glow of welcome.

When he is not there,
I really feel a little lonely,
sort of empty.
You know how it is!
You come home all expectant and
the little red dot on the answer machine
is absolutely still!!
Not blinking!! Cold and non-communicative!!
A very empty feeling.

YOUR GIFTS

Pretty, precious perfume bottles,
tiny gifts of thoughtfulness.
Though they do eventually stand empty,
a very strange thing occurs.
A woman cannot give up
a precious, tiny perfume bottle.

Each is imbued with memories
that soar on the barest waft of a scent.
Each can instantaniously
trigger a lifetime of memories.
Thank you for the many additions
to my collection.
Thank you for you.

THE BRACELET

22 hearts
or
22 birds linked in flight.
Smoth to the touch
are they.

An intricate weave
of gold.
Two ropes
it seems;
High gloss and dull.

The weave of
a life
into another.
The link of
2 hearts perfectly meshed.

Thus,
I shall wear
"Our hearts on my sleeve,"
linked at my wrist,
on
the pulse of my heart.

THE GIFT

The magnificents of it.
How unexpected.
The warmth,
yet cool clarity.
The depth,
so sophisticated.
The serene strength.
The solidity.
The magic.

Because it was yours,
as it is now mine,
it will live forever. Live on loving
hands, touching the lives of others,
sharing the life and memory of you.
May I be as fortunate as to find a
caring, concerned, appreciative
recipient,
when it is my turn to pass
the gift of the amethyst.

AN ALMOST SUMMER EVENING

The weather dictated I should sit on the patio
for an early supper.
The Quail are sounding.
The sun has not set.
There is no wind.

The sounds of distant high altitude silver planes,
the winged birds-all shapes, all sizes;
colors, views, privacy, peace
pervade my patio.

If someone were sharing my meal,
I would have to answer the question:
"No, the butcher swore this was not salmon
but fillet of red trout."
(I pouched it earlier and am serving
it cold with caper/lemon/mayonnaise).
You could fool me:
looks like, tastes like, but isn't salmon!!
The brussel sprouts are perfect.
The french roll toasted and simple.

*I brought out the book on tape.
I'm reading, but haven't turned it on.
It is too comfortable, just sitting and listening.
(I hope the neighbor isn't going to grind
the air conditioner all summer, 'cause
of course, I hear the condenseer).
However, peace still pervades and I could still
hear a Quail even in a disco.
I know and love its sound so well.*

*Yellow bellied black winged birds
just flew over.
Again they flew.
The sun's reflection makes them golden with
one half a moon above their path of flight.
The weather dictated I should sit on the patio
for an early supper.
The Quail are sounding.
The sun has not set.
There is no wind.*

*The sounds of distant high altitude silver planes,
the winged birds-all shapes, all sizes;
colors, views, privacy, peace
pervade my patio.*

If someone were sharing my meal,
I would have to answer the question:
"No, the butcher swore this was not salmon
but fillet of red trout."
(I pouched it earlier and am serving
it cold with caper/lemon/mayonnaise).
You could fool me:
looks like, tastes like, but isn't salmon!!
The brussel sprouts are perfect.
The french roll toasted and simple.

I brought out the book on tape.
I'm reading, but haven't turned it on.
It is too comfortable, just sitting and listening.
(I hope the neighbor isn't going to grind
the air conditioner all summer, 'cause
of course, I hear the condenseer).
However, peace still pervades and I could still
hear a Quail even in a disco.
I know and love its sound so well.

Yellow bellied black winged birds
just flew over.
Again they flew.
The sun's reflection makes them golden with
one half a moon above their path of flight.

(continued)

After all, they knew the rules.
You're on your own.
I will give occasional water,
but rarely nutrients.
If you cannot live with this,
then you are out and will be
replaced with some
young, fresh, healthy, vibrant, blooming
plants!!
No gold watches or insuraance here.

My goodness, the moon has moved.
How did that happen?
I'm still sitting here.
Is it because the sun has left?
Indeed, I can barely see to write.
At least it's only moved, not grown;
and is sill one half of itself.

I will have to continue at another time.
Perhaps we can talk about
the beginning of a summer evening,
beyond the twilight.
I think I shall now listen to my book.

UNDER THE SILKS

Wrapped in lace it was,
the shore.
Waves broken
far, far below;
shattered, spreading,
gathered, woven:
a piece of
Venetian lace!!

It is said,
a lost art,
this weaving of lace.
Such detailed patterns.
No two seascapes alike,
as in a snowflake,
Venetian lace.

And
deep below
this wrap of lace,
in intricate layer
after layer, after layer,
lies the depth of
the ocean scape.

*Even as I climb,
perspectives altered
minute,
by second,
by heartbeat,
the colored silks
lift me
beyond mind think.*

*One cannot escape
the majesty of God's plan.
How do we come to this place?
This awareness of
that which transcends
mundane
chores and pure existence?*

*Perhaps from the passion
of music,
of love,
of service;
from the awareness of
a greatness beyond self.
The perspective
under the silks.*

*Under the colored silks,
high above the mighty ocean,
(where many a time
I was rolled by these
locy, foam-like coverlets),
I could see
the contrast,
find the perspective.*

*The colored silks
with their hot pinks, purple,
yellow, orange,
and just a touch of reality white,
continue to lift me.
Below,
the coconut palms,
thatched canopy huts,
the walking railroad on the sand.
The skimpy boats,
the ant-like people
push me from them.*

(continued)
Above,
the full flower moon
and three stars.
Far, far beyond
continues
the majesty of God's plan.

For some brief moments,
I am captured, enraptured;
afloat between
the Heavens and the Sea.

I see the flag,
hear the whistle,
pull the cord
and
drop to earth.

Parasailing in Ixtopa

RANDOM THOUGHTS FROM MY WALK

Who am I?
Who am I, now that

I'm no longer
someone's wife,
no longer
someone's daughter,
no longer
someone's mother?
Who am I now?

I am I.
I am I alone with myself.
Does that feel O.K.?
I think so.
I'm getting used to it.
I'm liking it.
I'm feeding on myself, searching inward;
separating fantasy from reality.

It's very interesting what happens to a person who is all alone at the end of the day with nobody physically there. Talking on the phone doesn't count. In REALITY, the dial tone returns, FANTASY goes. In REALITY you are still alone. What you recall from the phone call cannot be touched, heard or seen. The sudden silence and emptiness could be overwhelming. The mind must control the heart at these times, or one could get very sick and depressed.

You must get out of yourself. See the bigger picture. Climb to the top of a mountain and survey the wonders; walk; talk to friends; volunteer; have company for a meal that you cook; garden; go somewhere new and different; write down your thoughts; exercise; read a great book; go to a movie, concert, football game; take a course; learn a craft or a new sport; go to church; dance; travel; listen to music; and on and on. There is so much out there. Participate fully.

You may still go home alone. But with a full life, it will be by choice and desire. So remember this, if there comes a time when your choice is to have someone there again, you are still alone, but at this point in time, sharing the aloneness of yourself and absorbing the aloneness of the other.

CHANGE OR CONTENTMENT

*They are content to dwell in the ugliness
of the known peramiters,
so as not to risk the unknown;
the possible beauties of the horizon,
of the ever broadning ripples,
started by the stone of wonder,
the pebble of challenge.*

*Content to wallow in comfortable;
afraid to dare, afraid to ask, afraid to change.
Oftentimes stuck in the quagmire of habit,
sucked down
deeeper and deeper into it,
'til bootstraps couldn't pull tthem out.*

*Who are they?
They are we.
We are "us", you and I in some form.*

ON WAITING

*Waiting is an acquired patience. Practice is the teacher.
Always have blank paper, pad and pen. Failing
that, a book to read. If really caught unprepaed,
close your eyes and take a memory break.*

*Try not to have waiting causse you distress or become a burden.
Make it work FOR you. Be grateful for the extra time.*

*There are different kinds of waiting;
some more stressful than others.*

*The Hospital waiting where a loved one is ill; or has
been in an accident; or is having an operation. You
wait and wait for the outcome. This is one of the more
difficult waits. This wait falls heavy on the heart,
like a great burden pressing down. The only relief is
talking to God, trusting in Him and the doctors.*

*You must not let fear of the unknown absorb this time.
Turn it over then rest and prepare yourself for what will
come: complete recovery, prolonged nursing and care, or
death. THEN when you know, go forward from there. Do
what needs to be done from that point, having prepared
through God's strength in your waiting moments.*

MORE BLESSED TO GIVE THAN TO RECEIVE

I have come to the conclusion that it is not only more blessed to give than to receive, but more necessary. There is a great yearning, a need to give, to have someone to love, to care for, with whom to share. It reallly isn't a process of wanting someone to love you or needing someone to care for you.

Let's see how that works. If you are totally alone, but healthy and employed, returning home day after day, to night after night alone, you will find yourself seeking out other humans. I am not going to get into animal substitutes as recipients of human love and needs.

These humans can be male or female. They fill an urgent need and become the conduit of your desire to give of yourself. It may be nothing more envolved than conversation. The need to hear your voice and see its acceptance or rejection on the face of the chosen human.

Don't get me wrong here. Isolation is necessary and a valuable source of creativiy, rejeneration, recovery, soul searching and growth. But it must be tested and balanced by other human beings for an individual to become the full wheel, smoothly turning, winding through the hills and valleys of life; passing over the ruts and sharp stones which life occassionaly drops in our path.

A NEW YORKER TYPICAL NONSENSE POEM

*Driven to
and from
starvation;
prisoner of the
Sausalito;
hiding in the
sunlight.
Druids dredged
in fog.*

*Lamp lights glimmer,
dim and glimmer.
Moonlight takes
the primal seat.
Must I rise and
take my stand,
or forever
ride the waves?*

*Prisoner of
the Sausalilto.
Ferried to and fro,
back and forth.
Hiding in the sunlight.
Captured!
Now, at dusk,
I feel I must
Rise up!
Cry out for freedom!*

DAY AND NIGHT

*I am writing this under my waterfall, watching
the large orange sun drop over the mountain. This
is an unbelievable oasis, utterly tranquil.*

*Now, the oaks stand silhouetted, the winged creatures dart
and swarm. The sun is dropping: 1/2 an orange, 1/4, a
tiny slice, it's gone. A sudden rush of coolness, twilight.*

*But still I stay and write. I am interrupted only by the sound
of the rushing, falling water. It follows it's pre-ordained
course, always caressing the same rocks at the same angle, and
now lies still in the pool below; only to collect itself for a final
surge down the last narrows to the really still reflection pool.*

*Now the path lights have come on, heralding the onset of
night. Twilight seeps through the sky, leaving only darkness.*

*Suddenly, there it is, working on fullness, but moving
ever so fast through the sky, the moon. I had lost it earlier
on in the trees. Frankly, I had forgotten about it with
all the other splendors. But now that the sky is quiet and
empty- no stars yet- the moon is softly there- just there.*

*And so I am reminded. I only miss you
on two occasions: day and night.*

MY CHRISTMAS MOUNTAIN

I'm on the top.
High noon in Westlake Village,
California, USA.

I have spoken with all those
who matter in my life.
Telephones are still a wonderfilled
means of communication.

A typical California Christmas.
The sun is so hot,
I have begun to peel off a layer of clothing.

And so I am reminded of
a sunny winter day in Colorado.
A first love and I
went cross country skiing with
picnic provisions:
bread, wine, cheese and two thous.

Don't ask!
I'm all alone on my
Chrisstmas Mountain.

Maybe it was the changing trail
I followed, or
the place where the path
ended with overgrowth.

Something.
Perhaps the dead still quiet,
not even car sounds this Christmas day,
brought me back to you.

(Continued)

*Back to the remembrance of you.
For now,
I know you have died.
So many loves die along the way.*

*But sitting on this new rock,
I choose
for a few minutes at least,
to have you live.*

*To bring back your lithe, lean body,
tanned by the winter sun.
You painted.
An artist, I recall.*

*Scarce as money was,
you took me "out to dinner" on
my 21st Birthday.
We did not take your panel truck.
I think it was broken.*

*I dressed for the occasion and
found myself
on the back of a motorcycle
you had to borrow.
Surprise!!*

*I think I fussed a bit,
my hair, the dress, the danger.
Seems I have been adjusting to
everyone elses' want to's ever since.*

*I may have adjusted myself
right out of any permanent
"have to" relationships for the
duration of my life on this earth.
Not so bad.*

(Continued)

*Total contentment
absorbs me this Day.*

*I woke leisurely at 7am,
stayed in my bathrobe 'til noon,
while opening my presents,
cooking a leg'o lamb,
listening to Richard Crooks
sing his glorious music.*

*On Christmas mountain,
I thought about the month of Advent
and the three Christmas Services at church.
I recalled all the Altar Guild events over
the year as I wrote my annual report.*

*The sun is dropping.
I need to get down this mountain
while I can still see
Wesstlake Village below me.*

*For two hours
there has not been a soul
within eyesight or earshot.*

*Tonight
I will join a dear lady and
her family for cocktails.
I will not stay for dinner.*

*Tomorrow,
I celebrate Christmas with
my parents,, sons, and grandchildren.*

*Another Christmas.
Surely, it is in my heart today.
But much more fully tomorrow.*

Christmas is meant for children.

HAVE YOU SEEN THE CROSS?

Have you seen the Cross
in the moonlight?
in the fountain?
on the mountain?

Yes, I have seen it
in the sorrow of the newly
baptised young adult with
no one to stand up with her;

in the face of the older woman
who had questions she had
for years been afraid to ask;

in the tired eyes of the father
running after an out of control
4 year old daughter.

Yes, I have seen the clear beauty of the empty silhoustted Cross,
the symbol of hope, of newness, rising up from the debris of
gathered sorrows, pains, loss, unanswered prayers, dumped at
its' feet, forming a reverse halo, as it were, circling its' roots.

It's as if unstrapping these knapsacks of burdens from our backs and laying them down at the foot of the empty Cross, adds to the power and strength of this Memorial Garden Cross. As the plants will grow with nurturing, sunlight, water, so too will this Cross grow in strength, power, significance from the prayers, the letting go of burdens and sorrows laid at its foot.

Have you noticed the growth?
Already the Cross has grown some copper.
And isn't it exciting and wonderful that this Memorial Garden Cross is user friendly? That it is outside, really well and beautifully lighted at night?
Available by sun, moon, fog, rain, wind; whenever the need moves one to be there.
No appointment.
Just go.

I have been there at night when neighbors are walking through our churchyard.
They are deep in intimate conversation, feeling safe and secure protected by the lighted Cross.

We have done something which for 16 years has been a dream, an EXTRA.

*In the beginning
we did it for us,
for the Women of Epiphany.
But,
I would like to suggest
that we will find the ripples of this Cross,
Fountain, and Memorial Garden,
spreading and circling into nooks and crannies
we had never foreseen.*

*Thank you God for giving us the vision and
fortitude to carry forth with your work.*

*Yes, I have seen the Cross
in the moonlight,
reflected in the fountain,
and on the mountain.*

Amen

www.ingramcontent.com/pod-product-compliance
Lightning Source LLC
Chambersburg PA
CBHW071459070526
44578CB00001B/386